See the Backpack

by Cameron Grieft
illustrated by Randy Chewning

Practice Decodable 1

Mc Graw Hill Education

Bothell, WA • Chicago, IL • Columbus, OH • New York, NY

MHEonline.com

Send all inquiries to:
McGraw-Hill Education
8787 Orion Place
Columbus, OH 43240

ISBN: 978-0-02-140709-5
MHID: 0-02-140709-6

Printed in the United States of America.

7 8 9 CTM 23

See the  .

paste

See the  .

crayons

See the  .

paper

See the  .

pencils

See the  .

books

See the  !

backpack